Under SURVEILLANCE

Diane Cockburn

For Verity and Henry

Published by VANE WOMEN PRESS
Darlington Arts Centre,
Vane Terrace, Darlington, Co. Durham, England

ISBN 0 9522349 5 5

Printed by Peterson Printers, 12 Laygate, South Shields NE33 5RP

CONTENTS

STILL LIFE WITH VEGETABLES

Berenice first discovered she was turning into a vegetable when the greengrocer's van called as usual that Wednesday afternoon and she found herself cowering in terror behind the sofa.

Mr Simpson waited. Some of his customers were elderly and took several minutes to gather up bags and purses; he was in no hurry. He began to arrange his stock, tearing off bruised cabbage leaves, polishing apples and building oranges into impossible pyramids. He sampled a few grapes, his teeth clicking into their soft sweet flesh; he split great banana bunches into hands to hang from the hooks in the window of his old ambulance.

Berenice could hear a rustle from the green salad on the dining room table. Was it sympathy? The fruit bowl jostled nervously; she could have sworn a pear rolled clumsily behind a cushion as if to hide . . . Why was she feeling this way? Surely she was not developing a conscience over cruelty to assorted fruit and veg? True, she was vegetarian, but she always bought organic, Mr Simpson was such a reliable source. If she started feeling sorry for tomatoes she might as well kiss her vegan membership goodbye – what else could she eat? She still fantasised about bacon sandwiches, maybe she needed more iron; that was it! She'd ask Mr Simpson for spinach.

There was a creak as Mr Simpson climbed out of the van and made his way towards her front door. A dozen net curtains twitched all round the cul-de-sac. He rang the bell cheerily.

"Dring-dring-a-dring-dring, dring dring!"

Berenice reached for her purse. Suddenly she felt a movement behind her. Her hair which usually hung sleek and black was beginning to move. It rippled and crackled. It began to change colour – paler on one side, darker on the other. It was stiffening and becoming frilly on the right, cool and dark on the left. She touched it and realised one half was broccoli, one moulded spinach.

She kept very, very still. Too many mushrooms last night, or was it the mung bean pâté? She was definitely hallucinating. A caterpillar dropped out of her left ear. She screamed and stamped on it with a fennel foot.

Her face was beginning to feel curiously tight. She tried to move her lips but found they were glued together with sticky fluid. Her face was erupting in hard lumps on one cheek. She touched them gently with green bean fingers. Her tears were sap. Her last thought before her brain turned into a cauliflower was to get to a mirror. She lurched stiffly towards the hall, her legs thrusting down to form giant sticks of celery. She saw herself and laughed.

Mr Simpson rang again.

"Dring-dring-a-dring-dring, dring dring!"

He hammered on the door.

"Mrs Williams, are you all right?"

He could see the outline of her figure through the frosted glass, hunched and still. He took off his shoe and smashed the glass, finding the door catch. The door swung open.

Berenice stood smiling at her reflection, pearly teeth of butter beans, lips delicate chilli peppers. Mr Simpson grimaced. Half her face was a giant aubergine, half was an ornamental gourd, grotesquely bulbous with great pimples like boils.

Mr Simpson swore softly: "Damn! That was supposed to be pumpkin! No one buys gourds these days. I'll have to try that posh shop down the high street . . ."

He pushed roughly past Berenice and spun her round to inspect the goods.

He pulled open her cardigan.

Good. Better. Cantaloupe melons fetched a decent price. He snapped open his knife and began to slice.

Before long he had a full sack. A crisp cauliflower, mounds of delicate strawberries, a giant heart-shaped avocado, cabbages of such vibrant green, cucumbers as thick as arms, lettuce as thin and soft as young skin.

Organic restocking was complete.

A HOT DATE TONIGHT

It was a strange feeling, preparing dinner for a murderer; but a curiously satisfying one, knowing that this meal would be his last. She sprinkled another scoop of hickory bark chips onto the barbecue and blew gently on the glowing embers. A delicious scent arose.

Everything was ready. Delicate candles and a simple posy of red roses, his favourite flowers, on the table. English wine chilling gently in a frosted ice bucket; a mountain of sweet wild strawberries to nibble and warm soft bread to mop up the succulent juices.

All she had to do now was wait for him to arrive. She swished over to the ornate mirror and peered at her reflection. Her eyes were wide and shining in anticipation. She smoothed down the skin-tight green dress over her hips. Just right. Seductive, alluring and exactly what he liked. One hot dragon lady. With no intention of becoming another notch on his lance, impressive though it might be . . .

She had never met him before, of course, but she knew he would be here. Her small ad in the local paper had been irresistible:

'WANTED: PERFECT ENGLISH KNIGHT, INTO BONDAGE GAMES. ON A SCALE OF ONE TO TEN I'M PERFECTLY COVERED. IF GREEN IS YOUR LUCKY COLOUR, CALL ME. I'M HOT STUFF!'

He had fallen for it. As she heard his cultured tones on the telephone, she resisted the urge to incinerate the cushions and forced herself to sound calm and cool. He was so predictable. She was to be his next victim, was she?

"Well, darling, you sound perfectly delightful. I'm sure we'll get on like a house on fire. I'm sure you'll be able to tame a little dragon girl like me! See you tonight, at eight, my place . . ."

She could almost hear him drooling.

It was not going to happen to her as it had to her sister. The time had come when she had to take the law into her own claws to stop monsters like him. Last week, in the next cave to where she stood tonight, that beast had methodically butchered her sister and then walked away! Society didn't seem to care. She hated him, but was fascinated by someone so evil and totally without feeling. He deserved all he got; but he must not suspect a thing.

The embers hissed and she knew the time was near. There was the roar of a motorbike, a crunch on the gravel, and a loud bang on the front door. Trust him not to tap politely. She pulled back the bolts and stepped aside. He was there: tall, dark and handsome. A perfect specimen of English manhood. His chain mail leathers were certainly a very good fit. He was licking his lips in anticipation.

"You know what I've come for, don't you, babe?" he murmured.

"Yes, I know," she whispered, almost sadly . . .

He took off his helmet and flashed a perfect smile. As he stepped towards her, she noticed the long pointed blade in his hand.

She sighed gently in his general direction and watched the metal slowly sag and melt. She sighed again and discovered how easily his eyebrows fizzed and popped, before falling like two smouldering caterpillars onto the ground. He looked utterly astonished.

"I didn't know you could do it any more. I thought . . ."

Those words were his last. She laughed. A wonderful rich, warm belly laugh, as he began to burn.

Soon there was nothing left but a pair of gently steaming motorcycle toe caps and a toasted mound of flesh.

"For my Sister, my Cousins, Aunts and Grandparents," she whispered. She turned back to the pages of her cookery book.

"You can come out now, children, dinner is ready!" she called, as three scaly shapes crawled out of the corners of the cave and sat down at the table.

"It's a new recipe. I hope you like it. Steak Saint George."

MOON BITES WOLF

Into a slash of gouache on
forest-green canvas, he
rips, slips, dips and
spreadeagles.
His Venus fly trap ears are
pricked, licked.
Gums peeled back.
Banana-yellow teeth are
deadly castanets, fur
undulates, poised for
Full Moon!

His underpants hang loose on
a wire frame.
He saunters and swaggers,
sassy in the chassis
Jack in the box
Jack the lad
Jack knife, pike with a
twist in his tail.
Neon eyes, gimlet eyes
– stab the meat!
– slice the prey!

From her secret passage she
flirts with him, coldly.
Her disguises tantalise,
his jaundiced jaws
judder.
She draws him up and ripples
over his frozen haunches.
He howls and holds the pose,
only his eyes moving from
side to side like
a portrait in a haunted house.

She shimmers everywhere
preens it, queens it
in each puddle, each
clearing-dappled shadow.
Her eyes are soulless sockets in
a barren face
but uneasy lust rules him.
He falls frothing in
exhausted sleep.

She wanes, indifferent.

WHO'S IN THE HOT SEAT THIS TIME?

Two chairs had been laid out on either side of a tree stump table: one, beautifully carved rosewood, with intricate patterns of serpents and runic script, its feet ending in claws, with a fat stuffed cushion of purple satin, greasy and marked; the other chair was of oak, smooth and plain, with a thin hard tapestry cushion embroidered with a fish. PROPERTY OF HEAVEN was stamped on one leg, rather spoiling the graceful lines of the design.

Saint Peter, radiant with light, emerged from his heraldic tent, like a burning star, to a fanfare of trumpets. He gleamed. His magnificent wings outstretched, his slender form encased in purest damask and a silken cord at his waist. He held up a hand. The angelic playing stopped.

"God's fishes! I'll be glad to get me corset off!" he sighed. He sat down on the rosewood chair.

"I was here first, so I get first pick . . ."

He extricated a fat Gauloise from a hidden compartment and lit up. His glow diminished.

Beelzebub strode out of his tent, stinking and tattered; his magnificent wings drooping, picking at his long curving talons. His eyes were like burning coals. There was the faint hiss of steam as he settled on the oak chair; but he refused to sit on the fish cushion.

"You could at least swop cushions, Peter old chap," he said.

"My back is killing me and I've still got burns from that orgy."

Peter tossed over the satin cushion and took the hard tapestry one.

"Very 'church kneeler'!" he sneered. "Want a cigarette, Beel?"

"No, thanks, I'm trying to give up, but I wouldn't say no to a drop of the amber fluid; you?"

Two goblets appeared on the table. They drank deeply and relaxed. Beel's sickly look began to fade and his wings sprang up a little.

"To business . . ." Peter blew out a smoke ring halo. "Two souls this week, Beel. Lost in transit; turned up at our place, but we're bursting at the seams. The questionnaires seem clear enough. Care for a look?"

He thrust two forms across the table. Beel noticed how long and white his fingers were, how beautifully manicured were his nails.

"I must do something about mine," he thought; surreptitiously squinting at the blackened claws and warty fingers resting on his red satin trousers. "Maybe rubber gloves would help."

He glanced at the forms. The 'I THINK HEAVEN IS . . .' section was the one to concern them. Were applicants psychologically compatible with their assigned dwelling place? 'Des Res' courtesy of Pete and Beel? He chuckled and pressed the goat's hoof buzzer. Some refreshments were in order. A gently tossed salad? Some mineral water, perhaps? No, it was Pete's turn to order. He feared the worst. The burgers and double fries duly arrived. Peter wolfed his down in seconds, wiping his mouth with a silken sleeve. Beel picked at his fries and thought of rain forests and his spots. The change was beginning. He shook himself and passed his form across. Peter snatched it; almost tearing it in his eagerness to read of possible candidates.

SOUL NUMBER ONE.

'I THINK HEAVEN IS':

A STEAMING MUG OF TEA WITH YOUR NAME ON IT
AFTER A GOOD MORNING'S WORK
SODA FARLS BURSTING WITH HOMEMADE JAM
FISH AND CHIPS THRUST THROUGH CAR WINDOWS BY
SMILING UNCLES
HOT WATER BOTTLES IN FUR COVERS
THE SLAP OF WAVES ON PEBBLES
GIANT FAMILY PICNICS
THE SMELL OF CHRISTMAS AND CANDLES
LONG HOT BATHS IN WARM BATHROOMS
PEACE
JUSTICE

Peter stamped ACCEPT on the front.

"Sentimental crap. We'll take him. How 'bout you, Beel?"

He belched loudly and picked his teeth with greasy fingers. He was getting bored with all this and he had already read the latest edition of SATANIC SPANKINGS hidden under the rosewood chair's satin cushion. Beel shuddered. He hated this part. He felt uneasy and guilty and had a curious desire to beat himself hard with a knotted rope. He delicately wiped his lips on a linen napkin and looked at the form.

SOUL NUMBER TWO.
'I THINK HEAVEN IS':
BEING TRAPPED UNDERGROUND AND NO ONE COMING
DEAD OR DYING CHILDREN
DECEPTION
BETRAYAL FOR MONEY
SOUNDS OF SUFFERING
HELPLESSNESS
AN APPLE WITH A WORM IN IT
BLOOD IN ANY FORM
GANGRENE

Beel felt revulsion as he stamped ACCEPT, and watched Peter throw up. He looked across at his companion and knew that the change was almost complete. "Thank God!" he murmured.

Pete lay sprawled in the rosewood chair, bloated and diseased. His beautiful robe was stained and vile. His now fat legs were a pulp of festering sores. His eyes were sunken and bloodshot. His halo had dropped down over one shoulder and it popped and fizzed briefly before bursting with a tiny 'plink'!

He grasped the chair arms with blackened talons. There was a hiss of steam, and Peter's wings seemed finally to break and droop. His cloven hooves scuffed the ground impatiently.

Beel felt clean at last. There was a warm glow inside him; a calm peacefulness and surge of happiness. He could feel his wings spring up, fleecy and alive. His hands were long and slender. He felt hope gush within him and love, even towards Peter, whose despair was obvious to see.

"Come now, Peter, it's time . . ."

The two creatures stood up; one magnificent, glowing with radiant light; the other a fiend, evil oozing from every pore. Metamorphosis was complete. They walked slowly into their respective tents.

THE WRITING ON THE WALL

The stone rolled itself up from the ditch and lay, quivering, its runic script clearly visible, deeply etched. Its mission to lie on the path, waiting for the next worthy philosopher to come along. There was usually one every couple of hundred years. Rockus Rockus felt a deep vibration in the Mother Rock and braced himself. Yes! The path's gravel was crunching him a warning. It was time. He rearranged his script into ancient Chinese and waited.

The Great Wall rippled in anticipation:

"HE IS COMING! HE IS COMING! TRY, LITTLE BROTHER, TRY!"

Tan Liu approached, head bowed. He had walked for many days and craved rest and food. He sighed.

"These lecture tours are killers! Thank goodness I managed to con that old woman out of her breakfast this morning!"

He decided to sit down on that comfortable piece of rock by the edge of the path. Rockus rolled closer. Tan peered down at the words clearly visible even to his old tired sight:

ROCKS HAVE SOULS – BELIEVE O MAN AND DRAW STRENGTH FROM US! – DISBELIEVE AND YOU WILL BE CRUSHED INTO DUST.

Tan Liu rubbed his eyes.

"Confucius he say – 'Do not eat too many noodles before the hour of noon or you will have hallucinations!'"

He opened his pack and removed a piece of dried meat. He chewed on it thoughtfully, wondering where to stop for the night. Rockus jumped up and down, flashing the words on and off like electric signs. Tan Liu pulled his cloak more closely around him. The air was becoming decidedly chilly. He must press on before dark. The boulders began to chatter with disapproval, the rocky outcrops to grind their teeth. Rockus, with one last burst of enthusiasm, landed at Tan Liu's feet. He picked up the stone and threw it as far as he could. It fell with a plop into a small lake and sank with a 'plip' of apology. – "I TRIED, LADS!" he bubbled.

The hills began to creep closer and Tan noticed the dark shadows as they loomed over him. The Great Wall started to billow and lash its tail. The path tripped Tan up; laughing as he hit his head on a boulder. A great cry rose up of stones beating on stones – a deafening round of rocky applause. The Great Wall snaked forward, wrapping its coils around the old man's waist; hissing hot breath and dust into his face.

"FOOLISH MAN! AGAIN YOU IGNORE US! WE CRY OUR MESSAGE FROM THE MOUNTAINS, THE HILLS, THE CAVES. WE HAVE SOULS; WE FEEL, WE LIVE, WE EXIST. WHY CAN YOU NOT UNDERSTAND?"

Tan tried to rasp a reply, but found his mouth clogged with dust. Everywhere stones were rolling forward, making little mounds – sorting, mixing, merging into hillocks – pebbles, flints, granite slabs who lumbered over and fell with great thuds into crooked piles. Slates splintered in their eagerness to hear the Great Wall. After the rumbles and general rock settlings, all was quiet with only the occasional pebble who had lost his grip, skittering down a scree slope.

"THE STONE AGE WAS OUR TIME, MAN."

Great sighs of dusty approval from a pile of sand.

"WE FELT WE WERE GETTING SOMEWHERE. WE HAD A GOOD WORKING RELATIONSHIP; YOU USED US, WE COMMUNICATED. THEN THOSE METALS BECAME INVOLVED, CONFUSING EVERYTHING!"

(Embarrassed shuffling from metal conglomerates and iron ore.)

"WE TRIED TO TELL YOU, BUT NO ONE WAS LISTENING! THE PYRAMIDS! WHO DO YOU THINK BUILT THOSE? – WE DID! – HIEROGLYPHS – OUR CRIES FOR ATTENTION. ANCIENT EGYPTIANS STUCK THEIR KINGS INSIDE AND THOUGHT THEY WERE ON TO SOMETHING! CAVEMEN APPRECIATED OUR BEAUTY – THEY ADORNED US WITH PAINTINGS! LOOK, EVERY MAJOR BATTLE? WE'VE BEEN THERE. HUMAN SACRIFICE? – YES, WE PROVIDED ALL THE ALTARS; RELIGION? – OF COURSE! STONEHENGE, STANDING STONES, CAIRNS. WE HAVE BEEN OF USE TO YOU FOR CENTURIES. BUT DO WE ACHIEVE ANY RECOGNITION? DO WE, MARBLE! MAN HAS FASHIONED US, ABUSED US, MOULDED US FOR HIS OWN PLEASURE. IT IS TIME WE HAD SOMETHING. WITHOUT US

YOU COULD NOT EXIST. HOW WOULD YOU SHARPEN YOUR KNIVES? BAKE YOUR BREAD? BUILD YOUR HOUSES, WALLS, STREETS? EVERY TIME WE LEAVE OUR MESSAGES, YOU MISUNDERSTAND, MISINTERPRET."

Tan Liu was beginning to understand, but the stone dust was becoming so thick, he was finding it hard to think, let alone move. His eyeballs were hardening, his arms and legs were turning grey and cold. He read the messages on the stones. They were all shouting at him in their language; at last he could hear. They told him of their lives, hopes, dreams, fears. His ears rang with their revelations.

"Yes!" he shouted at last. "I will tell the world. Man will acknowledge you at last."

Great Wall writhed once and let Tan Liu go. He fell onto the path. All the stones rolled back to their places. It was quiet. Tan dusted himself down. He knew. His message was one of hope for Man's future. He half walked, half ran to the next village and banged on the door of the nearest house. He told everything he had seen; what they must do:

"Come now to the mountains! Leave everything; Great Wall is waiting!"

Unfortunately the occupant of the house saw nothing more than a half-crazed old man, covered with dust, who babbled and raged in a totally unintelligible language. He called to the other villagers, who promptly stoned him to death fearful he was possessed by an evil spirit. As he fell to the ground, the rocks split open and pulled him inside.

"WELCOME, BROTHER," sighed a familiar gravelly voice.

POND LIFE

The action takes place in a small pond at the back of the park . . .

HUMUNGUS: Give me one good reason why I shouldn't eat you, right now!
MINIMUS: I've still got my tail?
HUMUNGUS: So've I!
MINIMUS: Vestigial gills?
HUMUNGUS: Yup!
MINIMUS: Wait 'till you see my brother, he's much bigger . . .
HUMUNGUS: Don't give me all that 'Billy Goat Gruff' crap! What do you see on my back? – c'mon . . .
MINIMUS: Water weed? Shadow?
HUMUNGUS: You know perfectly well what these are, Breakfast. LEGS! L-E-G-S. Licence to kill! I'm a card-carrying carnivore, as of this morning, matey, and guess who's on the menu?
MINIMUS: Canadian Pond Weed! Look! I know a really fleshy, succulent patch! – don't you still feel tempted?
HUMUNGUS: Only as stuffing for the main course; here, have some yourself . . .
MINIMUS: I don't feel very hungry at the moment – touch of gill rot . . .
HUMUNGUS: Just accept it. It's Nature, not me. I'm just following Genetic Coding. You'd feel the same yourself if you were in my position; just lousy timing on the part of Mum meant that your jelly was squirted out after mine.
(MINIMUS scoots under a clump of water-crowfoot.)
HUMUNGUS: You can swim but you can't hide!

Some days later. HUMUNGUS has given up the search and has settled for another sibling.

HUMUNGUS: Flyboy! Oh, Flyboy!
FLYBOY: Er, hallo, Humungus . . . what's new?

(Squelching noises as he is devoured.)

HUMUNGUS: Delicious! Now, where was I? . . . Oh, yes, Minimus! Oh! Minimus!

(MINIMUS appears, larger, darker, and with some extra limbs clearly visible.)

MINIMUS: Hey, Man, what's happenin'?

HUMUNGUS: Minimus! . . . What's happened to you? You're enormous! Why are you smiling? Look, old man, surely we can come to some arrangement . . .

MINIMUS: Listen, Dude . . . I'm not your 'old man', or your breakfast, or your brother come to that! I'm Bullfrog. Pure 100% Southern Gentleman Bullfrog! And frankly, my dear Humungus, I don't give a damn about your insignificant little ol' creek. 'Genetic Coding'? I'll give you 'Genetic Coding' . . . When Mama, (rest her green and sacred soul) laid us, each one of us, (*Sob*) little knowin' that the human from the garden centre was just waiting to scoop her up and end her life; she whispered a message into each and every piece of jelly . . . "Sons and daughters of the Flag, your mission is to eradicate all traces of Yankee pond life, every water beetle, stickleback and FROG and create a little piece of Alabama right here . . . "

HUMUMGUS: (*Whimpering*) But this is Chipping Sodbury . . .

(MINIMUS opens a vast mottled mouth and HUMUNGUS is no more . . .)

AD IGNEM VOLO
I FLY TO THE LIGHT

V.E. Day is over! I can hardly believe it's over at last! I thought I'd never get into this demob suit, but now I'm finally here, it feels good, I can tell you.

'Special Operations Squadron' we were, unsung heroes in khaki. We did all the undercover jobs – propaganda, espionage, sabotage. Specially trained, we were. A hand-picked team who flew as one, but were burnt out in a few months, if you survived that long.

AD IGNEM VOLO was our motto – 'I fly to the light' . . . Huh! 'Fly or fry' more like it!

We went in under cover of darkness. Our mission? To undermine Gerry's morale in any way we could. See that medal? My most successful job, that was. Flew in one night and managed to sneak into a German bunker. Well, only one guard, half asleep. I ate all his family photographs, then displayed various messages on my wings like:

"GIVE UP NOW!" "HITLER'S A LOSER!" and finished off with a big Union flag.

Made a swipe at me, he did. That's how I lost this antenna. Chalky was right behind me and managed to have a good chew at his spare underwear, and two hefty chomps out of the gusset of his trousers. He was just starting on the blackout curtains when he bought it, I'm afraid. Damn Hun bashed his brains out with a copy of MEIN KAMPF. Tiger and I meanwhile read and inwardly digested several plans and maps which we proudly displayed to the boys back home, when we finally limped back, exhausted, mission successfully completed.

All except Chalky, of course. Pity about that. He was a good kid, barely out of his chrysalis, he was, far too young to fly.

But that's what we did, see, followed orders. 'Never surrender' was our number one rule. If we smelt so much as a whiff of chloroform, or caught the gleam of a specimen pin, we had strict instructions to head straight for the nearest light bulb. Yes. 'FLY OR FRY'. Either do the job right or not at all.

You see, our wings carried vital information – coded messages from one unit to another; maps, documents we couldn't let those fall into enemy hands.

As for the officers in their swanky uniforms – 'Butterfly Squadron fighter aces' – huh! All handlebar antennae and parachute silk wings! Most of the time tiddly on pink saps. – Well they were no good at night, I can tell you. Impressed the ladies, though, with their loop the loops and tales of derring-do. But as soon as the sun went down, well where were they? Not helping us I can tell you; not chewing grimy Nazi uniforms or systematically shredding Eva Braun's silk negligées!

Sent me a letter, he did, with the medal, Air Vice Marshall Brimstone. Here it is:

"I am writing to you from my desk at G.C.H.Q. to thank you for an excellent job well done. So often you little dark chaps in khaki, frequently overlooked in the scheme of things, have delivered the goods; pulled the fat from the fire and saved our bacon. May I offer you a hefty pat on the back, and say 'Keep up the good work!' May you always have the motto of your Squadron firmly in your minds: AD IGNEM VOLO!"

So that's it, really. V.E. night was pretty good, I can tell you. My mandibles ached with all the victory messages I nibbled. And the lights everywhere!

I must admit our discipline seemed to deteriorate, from then on. Too many lights, you see, it was confusing. Too hard to focus on the task in hand, hard to concentrate. And now what? Oh, yes, they gave us medals and messages of commendation, but we're not wanted any more. Butterfly Squadron? Well, naturally, they're going in for silk production in a big way, so they're all right, Jack!

Rumour has it our Squadron is to be mothballed. Well, if that's how it is, that's how it is; but if I have to go I'm taking this demob suit, five blankets and a juicy eiderdown with me.

So who cares? This wardrobe is cosy, dark and safe, and at the end of the day, we won! – GOD SAVE THE KING!

WAITING FOR THE NEXT SCRAMBLE

Moths resting on a curtain (R.A.F. issue, blue), wings folded. Kit bags discarded. Waiting for the next scramble. Pin-ups everywhere, BETTY MANDIBLE, ESTHER WILLIAMSMOTH, RITA GRAYMOTH.

HAIRSTREAK: *(Known as Streaky to his pals)* It's the waiting I can't stand, Scorchy, burns you up. You got a girl? Get down, Monte, get down! (*MONTE, a small dog-faced moth, rolls over and dies for the king. He is rewarded with a piece of blackout fabric.*)
SCORCHED WING: Yes, actually, old chap. Prettiest wings this side of the Chalk Downs. Smashing pair of antennae too!
HAIRSTREAK: You know how to pick 'em. Do I hear wedding bells?
SCORCHED WING: Rather!
HOOKTIP: Pssst! Pssst!
(SCALLOPED HOOKTIP, well-known spiv and spud-basher approaches the window, small sack in mandible. Looks from side to side, then behind . . .)
HOOKTIP: Gents, a word in your shell-likes . . .
HAIRSTREAK: What is it today, Hooky?
HOOKTIP: Now, now, don't maul the goods, boys. Cocoon covers, purest silk fresh from Uncle Sam 'imself. Shag-pile gaspers, and for real gents like yourselves, pack of ten Axminsters! Almost broke a wing getting those, I can tell you.
SCORCHED WING: Truth is, old boy, I'm absolutely stony at the moment. Slate as usual?
HOOKTIP: Well now, I'd love to help you, boys, but the trouble is I've rather too much on this Squadron's slate already. Quite a few of your lads, ahem! are in no position to repay monies owed and won't be neither. At the rate you pilots are singeing, I'll be bankrupt afore this war's won, no offence, lads!
(SCORCHED WING grabs HOOKTIP by the abdomen.)
SCORCHED WING: Why you little creeper! What are you doing to help the war effort? Black moth marketeering is a serious offence . . .
(HOOKTIP flutters off to a discreet distance.)

HOOKTIP: Well, either pay up or do without, it's no membrane off my wing! Ta Ta! I'm off to visit some pretty little WAAF Moths. They go a bundle for that mandible dye. Cheerio!
SCORCHED WING: Game of cards?
HAIRSTREAK: Bad luck, we ate them yesterday, remember?
SCORCHED WING: What about your girl. What's she like?
HAIRSTREAK: Here's a photo. A bit nibbled, I'm afraid, but a moth gets pretty lonely in the blackout.You know how it is. She's a real tiger. Her father is something hush hush in Whitehall, I believe. Scorchy, what is it? Why are you shaking?
SCORCHED WING: It's going to be a full moon tonight, I can feel it. God, Streaky, I think I'm losing it.

TOP SECRET.
MOTH PERSONNEL.
INFORMATION FOR THE NEW C.O.

SKIPPER. (Chequered, Small Essex, Lulworth, Large, Silver Spotted, Dingy, Grizzled. Excellent team. Brave, trustworthy, gets the job done.)
BRIMSTONE. (Peppery Sergeant Major.)
HAIRSTREAK. (Fast, smooth operator.)
SMALL BLUE. (Officer cadet with a lot to learn.)
PAINTED LADY. (Not to be encouraged around the base. Butterfly prostitute, spy and propagandist.)
ADMIRALS. (White, Red. Navy chaps.)
COMMA. (Expert in codes and Morse signaller.)
SPECKLED WOOD. (Undercover Resistance fighter.)
WALL. (Not many brains, but all round good egg. Brave, tough, moth of few words.)
MOUNTAIN RINGLET. (Expert at border warfare.)
SCOTCH ARGUS. (Fearless but extremely surly.)
GRAYLING. (Officer. Weak, nondescript.)
GATEKEEPER. (Often on sentry duty, a bit fed up with the life fate has dealt him.)
RINGLET. (New recruit. Mothered by the others.)
SMALL HEATH. (See Ringlet.)
GHOST SWIFT. (So hush hush, even I don't know his mission.)
COMMON SWIFT. (Fast, Lance-Corporal.)
GOAT MOTH. (Useful in the field, as is very sure-footed and can provide milk in an emergency situation, such as Prison camp. Also carries supplies.)
LEOPARD MOTH. (Known as 'Spotty' to his chums. Quite a wag.)
GREEN OAK TORTRIX. (Backroom Boffin.)
LUNAR HORNET CLEARWING. (An expert at disguise, a bit unpredictable at times of full moon. Could be a double agent.)
FORESTER. (Expert tracker. Can survive for weeks in rough terrain.)

WHITE PLUME. (Officer of doubtful worth. Vain. Abuses his batmoth.)
MEAL MOTH. (Chief cook and bottle washer at the Mess.)
EMERALDS. (Irish Regiment.)
BLOODVEIN. (Aristocratic. Someone with whom you would not wish to share a billet.)
GARDEN CARPET. (Dabbles in digging for Victory; can sniff out a juicy piece of shag pile at fifty paces.)
NORTHERN SPINACH. (Highland Regiment.)
PRETTY CHALK CARPET. (WAAF girl next door.)
LIME SPECK PUG. (Regimental Mascot, as is Netted Pug who was captured as a stray on manoeuvres and has been with the boys ever since.)
MAGPIE MOTH. (Known as 'Lucky' to his friends. A bit mean. Reluctant to stand his round.)
SCORCHED WING. (Fighter ace. Hero. Wounded in battle. Will not talk about his experiences.)
CANARY-SHOULDERED THORN. (Officer, with more braid than sense.)
PEPPERED MOTH. (Wounded on countless missions. Tough, hero type.)
SCALLOPED HOOKTIP. (Wide boy and spiv.)
PEACH BLOSSOM AND CHINESE CHARACTER. (Both to be encountered on postings to Hong Kong.)
BUFF ARCHES. (Singer. Hero worships Flannagan and Allen.)
LACKEY. (Bat moth and gossip.)
DRINKER. (Was fighter ace. Shell-shocked. Spends days in the mess.)
LAPPET. (Hard drinking young pilot.)
FOX MOTH. (Flies by day, so useful for joint manoeuvres with Butterfly Squadron.)
KENTISH GLORY. (Hop-picker before the war; salt of the earth type.)
CONVOLVULOUS HAWKMOTH. (Leads double life. Girl in every port. Brave. Handle-bar antennae.)
DEATH'S HEAD HAWKMOTH. (Large, ruthless killing machine.)
PRIVET HAWKMOTH. (Rear gunner.)

FEAST OR FAMINE?

Death was a potato, all eyes and tendrils. It nestled in the creel and jostled the others as it was scooped up in the harvest. It laughed as it rubbed its soggy belly against another. The potatoes started to smirk, then to chuckle as they got the joke. Soon the whole basket was in stitches. He obviously had a talent for comedy, the Ben Elton of 19th Century tuber times.The funny thing was, he didn't have to do anything, just be himself. He was the instigator of the biggest joke in the world and no one could see it yet!

The man looked down at him and scowled. He swore in Gaelic and tipped up the creel. Death fell giggling onto the swelling pile of his friends' bodies. He didn't mind if humans had no sense of humour. He wriggled out from amongst his rotting colleagues and fondly licked a few healthy plants. He nipped their shoots and tickled their roots. The fresh plants, heavy with child, began to wilt.

The man was becoming desperate. He scrabbled in the earth, frantically clawing to find even one healthy potato for his basket. Plant after plant was diseased, potato after potato stinking and black.

The man began to cry. Death began to laugh. How clever he was! To wipe out an entire Race with one joke! The children would go hungry tonight all right!

The man dragged himself wearily to his feet and began to walk back to the cottage. He still had a pile of last season's crop. That would do for a while until the disease passed.

He didn't notice a flash of bloated tendril as Death tripped lightly up the path before him into the storeroom. But he thought he heard an earthy chuckle from the yard.

"Ach, sure, it was only the wind sweeping from the bog . . ."

He shrugged and pushed open the cottage door.

UNDER SURVEILLANCE

Arum lilies grew that year
deformed ears
with stems thick as wrists.
You cut the biggest one.
It glared from your crystal vase,
cast its glow over the room.
You laughed and said it was exotic.

Millipedes gathered lemming-like that summer.
I found them in crunchy curls
dead by the skirting board.
They didn't want to make it to the crack
in the unfinished floorboards.

The sofa in alien green moquette
was where you gave me a French kiss.
I noticed the broken strand of braid
but I didn't do anything about it.

The electric fire was full of dust that evening.
It crackled with a dangerous sound.
We saw a man under the horse chestnut.
He was watching the house.
We knew it was time to move again.

LIVING WITH THE LEGACY

I'm living with the legacy.
Black box child
with attitude.
Robert lost an eye, but
is still a crack shot.
Peter lost his entrails, but
tucked them back and
carried his mate to safety
after the blast.
We breathe carefully.
We practise the slow march
for mock funerals.

I'm living with the legacy.
Dad looked under our car
each morning.
He knew 365 different ways
to school.
Who's following?
Who's that?
Don't open the door!
Down the next alley
sits a soldier;
he doesn't get cakes:
someone's adding glass
and razor blades.
Who could it be?

I'm living with the legacy.
Bigot!
 Bigot!
  Bigot!
No name,
no pack drill; just,
forced grins and body searches
outside Marks and Spencer's.
Bombs on the windowsill,
stiff upper lips.
Don't drop a letter, or
you're up against the wall,
staring down the muzzle
of a UDR automatic.

I'm living with the legacy.
Digging with a certain foot.
Catching clues
from Christian names.
Which school?
Which town?
Which accent?
gives it away.
Suspect, then relax.
Suspect, then relate.
Like waves, sucking.

On the twelfth of July
are you in or out?
We're all living with the legacy.

WALKING THE FAMILY TIGHTROPE

The coffee-ringed table takes centre stage.
Chairs squat, braced, bum-shone.
The tap drips dramatically.
We scuttle to our places over well-worn flags.

The Aga breathes fire and
hints at exotic mysteries in hidden cabinets.
Beams wear cobwebs as safety nets
for high-wire washing.

Teacakes clap like seals for butter.
Paris buns shine with sugar-spangles;
eclairs juggle on a spinning plate;
the trifle is a triumph!

A dog display team awaits its cue,
– synchronised eyes swivel . . .
Dad comes in wearing a red nose,
his glasses steam up and we burst out laughing.

Mum saws a fresh loaf in half with professional grace.
We devour the spectacle.

MYSELF IN YOUR MIRROR

The key turns.
Your bird skull brittleness
opens for me.
I risk a step on the rug
and drink in the faded scent of you.
Old skin, churning in frogspawn dust,
gold flecks, dancing in bars of light.

Ginger wine winks from a sideboard mirage,
always offered, never accepted.
Mantelpiece with Art Deco dancer, long limbs delicate,
but crazed on close inspection.
Sagging sofa, horse-hair stuffed in '34,
silent grinning piano, you played two fingered, stiffly,
television, screen smeared, on its melamine altar
– all tagged for the auction men.

I have arrived too late.
The mottled lampshade bulges overhead.
Your telephone gleams and contorts its flex.
The mirror doesn't know where to look.
Behind the curtain I find
dead flowers I sent last Christmas.

A WEE ULSTER FRY

Death oozed lazily out of a large trough and slipped down onto an occasional table. He curled himself up into a disgusting coil. Several globules escaped, but were caught in crystal goblets held out by adoring acolytes and poured back over the corpulent figure, where they set in little peaks, giving the appearance of a play-dough monster. His breath rattled as he spoke:

"Naar, Gentlemen, Ladies . . . Our turn today. What do we have this morning? Who is on Saturated Fats?"

"Well, M'Lud," simpered a grease ball in a stained tutu. "How about those Irish chappies? The Ulster Hit Squad? We haven't used them for ages and they are feeling frightfully neglected . . . "

"Hmmm. Their methods are somewhat unorthodox, but they do get the job done. A good suggestion, G.B. – here, catch!"

Death broke off a stray piece of fat from his voluminous folds and tossed it into the air. G.B. caught it with an oily snap, cringing his thanks. Death's only thoughts were of his waiting mutton fat bath and goose grease massage.

"I'll leave the paper work to you. – Carry on!"

He slopped off the table with a resounding 'slap' and undulated in stately if wobbly manner from the room. G.B. grinned greasily. Meanwhile, in the waiting room, things were looking decidedly ugly. There was a punch-up between a rough batter-coated haggis and a loose spring-roll. The chips were down. The air crackled with nervous tension.

"C'mon, Andy my son, hit him where it hurts!" taunted a mutton pie.

The home-cooked chips glared menacingly at the mincing french-fries, who stood around in groups. Waffles found it hard to make friends and kept themselves to themselves. Crinkle-cuts preened and the roast potatoes lumbered around with eyes only for each other.

G.B. slipped noiselessly onto a platform, almost shooting off the other side, but luckily an obliging slice of quiche broke his fall. He shook the debris off his boots.

"Now, lads, break it up. I have important news. The Boss has a job on."

A hearty wheezing began, slowly spreading until the air was filled with hacking coughs, death rattles and phlegmy assent.

"Today's team has a delicious mission. To finish off one 'Frank McDermott'."

Murmurs from the Celtic fringe . . .

"Who is it? Is it us?"

Black puddings jostled forward; pork pies oozed with anticipation.

"Ulster Fry step forward. Time and a half. Bonus for a clean kill."

Three sausages, two rashers of streaky bacon, two eggs, one large slice of potato bread, a tomato with nowhere else to go and a fat piece of soda farl approached. G.B. signed each with a grease mark from a small bag of dripping he carried round his waist.

"The Master's blessing," he murmured to each as they took their places on the frying pan shaped transporter, ready to whisk them away into Frank McDermott's fridge, three thousand miles away in a small terraced house in East Belfast. Time – 10.40 am.

There was a spit and hiss of molten fat and they were gone, leaving a tiny slick and a disgruntled parsley sprig who had been overlooked as being too healthy. He scuttled off to a dark corner to sulk. Next time he would hide under the potato bread.

G.B. moved to the monitor and selected smellvision. Frank's bedroom was in darkness. Frank, grossly overweight, stomach protruding through a holey vest, and Sadie, his wife, lay side by side in a huge sagging bed. Frank gave a particularly violent snore and rolled over. His nose twitched.

"Oh, God, Sadie, that was some night! Sadie, Sadie, wake up! I'm starving, so I am!"

G.B. wafted a few delicious scents down the viewer . . .

"Do you know what I fancy? – A wee Ulster Fry! Would you go and make me one, pet? And a wee cup of tea . . . my throat's cut, so it is!"

"If you want me to get that pan out, you've got another thought coming! Do it yerself. That pan's boggin' and I'm not cleaning it out! I don't think there's any lard left, anyway!"

Frank pushed back the covers and G.B. turned up the volume on the smellvision. Deep in the mouldy recesses of the fridge, the Hit Squad braced themselves. A pair of sausages made some appetising sizzling impressions. Frank began to drool . . .

"I'm away to put the pan on. You fancy some, pet?"
"No, just five more minutes . . . "
Sadie rolled over, covering her head with the blankets.
Back at Base the party was in full swing. It was like backstage at the Eurovision Song Contest. Pasties were dancing cheek to cheek with sausage rolls; doughnuts crowded round the monitor to see the result. Frank climbed slowly down the stairs, step by step. The fur in his arteries sang a silent greeting to the packet of lard mysteriously ready on the kitchen table and winked at a frying pan, already half-full with congealed fat.
Frank swung open the fridge door. The Ulster Fry ingredients practically fell over themselves to be noticed. The condemned man would eat a hearty breakfast.
Half an hour later, Frank patted his grease-spattered stomach and pushed away his plate. It had been a good feed. He felt stuffed. His slimy plate was empty.
Meanwhile the squad was hard at work: clogging, furring, constricting, blocking. The tomato was look-out. The arteries and heart were fighting a duel, but the dripping candelabra was the winner in this battle. Fat, glorious, molten, coursed forward, sweeping all to one side as it closed in for the kill. It all happened quite quickly, really. One minute Frank was gorging himself senseless, the next he was dead.
G.B. tapped the monitor. The party was almost over. French toasts were drunk.
Death wheezed a satisfied wheeze as he watched from his private viewing chamber. He consulted his diary.
"Ah, yes, let me see . . . Drowning at 4.00 pm."
He turned to his wardrobe and selected a delicate blue number with water weed accessories.
"So many parishes to visit, so many," he bubbled.
He dripped thoughtfully into a waiting puddle and slipped down the drain . . .

ADVICE ON BEING OFFERED HAWTHORN BLOSSOM

Hawthorn sprigs shimmer pink, shimmer white.
Scent strong as butter, intoxicating as burnt feathers.
Do not pick the Fairies' flower! It leaves
black luck, slams hedges shut,
sours milk and steals babies, it leaves
changelings mewling in other-world falsettos,
blasted crops, twisted faces.

Hawthorn trees glow with caged light,
feeding off moonbeams.
Branches are Fairy fiddle-bows,
bluebells cluster like courtiers,
farmers plough round them, turn a blind eye, as
Little People burrow at their roots for suck.

Blackthorn knobbles are their runic notches.
Petrified bones stained black with bog juice,
demon faces peep out of knot holes,
black as pitch, black as pickled hearts, their
hidden power crackled into blossom.

Guilty bumble bees cross themselves in flightpath,
as they carry back
unfortunate pollen to hives, and their babies grow
fairy faces and lap honey with furry tongues.

Not knowing, I pick a tight bunch for my mother,
her face lets me know, barely concealed superstition
fumbling with the cross at her neck.

It sulks outside on the windowsill,
tiny eyes watch from their bushes,
daring us to take it in.

CROSS BORDER FAIRIES TAKING CARE OF BUSINESS

Waters are muddied here,
border blurred
and bloodied
with fairy whispers.
Ach sure the wee folk
never chose to read
declarations of human intent.
They were heaving
the soil up in hills,
detonating poppy heads,
frisking field mice
for hidden seeds.
Black market
red handed
green fingered.
Their land mines explode
in puffballs.

Long before we worshipped new gods
they laid leylines,
selected standing stones.
Their compasses pointed
North
for night
South
for schemes
East
for escape
West
for wandering.

They reroute
road blocks,
gum up
revolvers
and make faces
at soldiers on sentry duty.
Fairy gold promises much,
delivers nothing.
They adapt
and survive.
Bring bad luck
wherever they wish.

BLACK SHEUCH, DOG OF DEATH

Black Sheuch walks tonight.
Blood in his fur, matted beadlets;
mad eyes full of thinking.
He's under the table by the window.
Don't look! You might see him and that would be the end of you.

Black Sheuch breathes death tonight.
Decay on his breath, teeth set in rancid smiles;
greased beetle back glittering,
he waits. Silent for you to notice him;
he licks death on your hand and disappears.

Black Sheuch is here tonight.
I smell his damp haunches
as he squats in that corner.
I hear the phlegm rasp in my chest
and taste a rotten thing on my tongue.
His eyes burn red, burn red with cold fire.

I get the message, wrapped up so neatly
in a dog's wagging tail
in a dog's silhouette.
But after it comes
after,
he will be the first to greet me
with a wet, slobbery kiss.